Coming In on a Wing and a Prayer

A Granddaughter Remembers Her Wartime Hero

By Kelly J. Brown

This book is dedicated to you, Grandfather.

I thank you with everything that is in me for the price you paid for my freedom.

The story of your life has been etched in my heart and will forever be there.

I love you.

SECOND PRINTING

COPYRIGHT © 2005, 2006 THE VISION FORUM, INC.

"Where there is no vision, the people perish."

THE VISION FORUM, INC.
4719 Blanco Rd., San Antonio, Texas 78212
www.visionforum.com

ISBN-10 1-929241-99-2
ISBN-13 978-1-929241-99-6

Scripture taken from the New King James Version®. Copyright © 1982 by Thomas Nelson, Inc. Used by permission. All rights reserved.

Design by Joshua Goforth

PRINTED IN THE UNITED STATES OF AMERICA

A Note from the Author

This is the story of my grandfather, William Brown. I have written this book in the style of a letter written by me as a grandmother, sometime in the future, to my future grandchildren about memories of my grandfather, their great-great grandfather, William Brown. My hope is that readers of all ages will see the story of my grandfather as a meaningful reminder of the importance and pricelessness of freedom. A sincere appreciation for the men of World War II cannot be felt without a clear understanding of that for which they fought. Men aren't telling it, the schools aren't teaching it, and the legacies that have been left by thousands of soldiers are being lost. I often wonder how my generation would respond if our country found herself in, say, a World War III. Would they be willing to sacrifice their lives for the principles for which America stands? Do they know what those principles are? Psalms 11:3 and 12:1b come to mind. "If the foundations are destroyed, what can the righteous do?" "For the faithful disappear from among the sons of men." Our country has begun to turn her face away from the foundations she was so firmly built upon long ago. Her foundations are being destroyed, and I find myself asking as the psalmist David did: "what can the righteous do?" The faithful are disappearing, but it is my prayer that the ones who are faithful will be encouraged by this letter. And maybe, as a result of this letter, others will become faithful.

Kathy J. Brown

Grandchildren,

    As I was going about some business tonight in my attic, I
stumbled upon a box full of youthful memories: old favorite
books, letters from old friends, and newspaper clippings I
had scribbled comments on--all from years ago.

    I enjoyed looking over these things, but after a few
minutes, they were returned to the old brown box, to be once
again put away. There was one memory retrieved, though, that
I feel must not be kept in a box--a pile of pages from an
old journal entry; covered in pictures from one of the most
significant trips of my life.

    Something deep down inside of me was whispering, "Pass this
on!" I believe this was a reminder from the Lord that all who
have stories to tell of God's faithfulness in their lives
have an obligation to pass them on.

    It would mean so much to me if you would look over this
entry--I have included it here, along with a letter that the
Lord has lead me to write. It brings tears to my eyes to think
that these memories have long been kept safe, kept away--but
they must now be made known.

    Yours faithfully,

    Grandmother

March 12, 2005

Today, I stood on the black sands of Iwo Jima with my grandfather. Sixty years ago, my grandfather was a twenty-year-old young man flying over this island on his bombing raids against the Japanese. Now, I am a twenty-year-old young lady coming back with him! Today, he flew over Iwo again—this time he didn't come to fight, he came to remember a story, a story of the sovereignty of God.

I'm so thankful for Grandfather's multi-generational vision. Because of that vision, I am able to stand in the same places he once stood; I am seeing the same sights he once saw—and I can hear the stories of men who gave up everything they had ever known, or ever wanted to know, so that I might live in freedom.

I stood there, looking out into the clear blue waters off the rugged shores of Iwo; the rhythmic sound of the waves rushing to the shore had my complete attention, and I began to imagine. Oh journal, I imagined a wedding, all pure and white—there was a girl covered by a veil. I imagined a young father with a daughter on his knee, singing, and laughing as they sat. I imagined a family—father, mother, daughters and sons—eating around a table; they were talking to each other of the events of the day. I saw a father fishing with his teenage son, discussing the details of life together, as they cast out and reeled in. All the things these men never had, because they wanted the future generations to be given such opportunities. As I thought of these things with Grandfather by my side—I was completely undone.

Papa, David, Grandfather, and I took this journey back in time with some dear friends and a small film crew—so that we could record the lives of the men who fought there. There were interviews taken

and pads of paper rapidly filled with scribbles. We were hungry— hungry for the stories. At the end of the day, we were full. God was good.

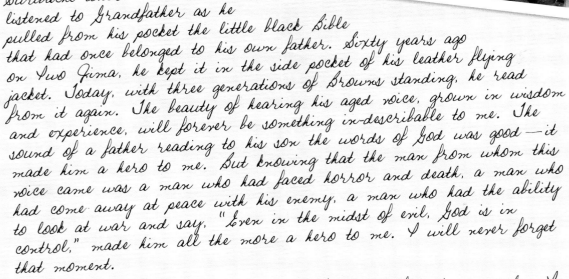

By the time the sun went down, I had ridden the dusty roads, walked the black shores, and climbed the ash of Mt. Suribachi where I stood and listened to Grandfather as he pulled from his pocket the little black Bible that had once belonged to his own father. Sixty years ago on Iwo Jima, he kept it in the side pocket of his leather flying jacket. Today, with three generations of Browns standing, he read from it again. The beauty of hearing his aged voice, grown in wisdom and experience, will forever be something in-describable to me. The sound of a father reading to his son the words of God was good—it made him a hero to me. But knowing that the man from whom this voice came was a man who had faced horror and death, a man who had come away at peace with his enemy, a man who had the ability to look at war and say, "Even in the midst of evil, God is in control," made him all the more a hero to me. I will never forget that moment.

What a legacy I will have to pass on! I pray for the day when I can tell these stories to my own dear children. Even now, I ask the Lord that He will make my children to have the most grateful hearts in the whole world. May they never forget the sovereignty of God in preserving the life of their forefathers; and in some way—may they, by knowing the story I will someday tell, live a more godly life because they've been inspired.

I'm tired now—it's been a long day. I'll close for now. More later.

Kelly

Great-Grandfather William at eight years of age

"This will be written for the
generation to come,

That a people yet to be created
may praise the Lord."

Psalms 102:18

Chapter 1

My dear Grandchildren,

   As I write to you, I am sitting here in my living room by
the fire, the yellow and orange colors of the blaze glowing
strong, and the crackling of the logs almost putting me
to sleep. So many thoughts come into my mind while sitting
here, many different stories and memories of days gone by.
One memory in particular I would like to share with you--a
memory that will fade if not passed on. This memory is of my
grandfather, your great-great-grandfather, fighting in World
War II years ago, in 1941! I can remember the stories he used
to tell me as a little girl about the planes he flew. He was a
pilot, you see.

   My grandfather had always loved to fly, even from the
time he was a little boy, so I will go back to before the
war, to the first time that William (that was Grandfather's
name) ever flew in a plane. He was only five years old when
a barn stormer (a dare-devil pilot who would buzz local farm
buildings) flew over his family's chicken farm in a biplane.

William's mother waved the plane down and asked the pilot if he would take her son on a short ride in exchange for a homemade chicken dinner. Of course, the man said yes! This changed little William's life, and from that day on, he had a love for flying. The year was 1927.

Two years passed and another major event occurred in William's life. The stock market crashed and the Great Depression began. Over the next ten years, more than thirteen million people would lose their jobs.

I believe, children, this was a time, even though we didn't know it, when our country was being prepared for the war to come. The Depression turned out to be a training ground for even harder times ahead. Families all over America learned how to do without many things to which they had become accustomed. As men became unemployed, children went to bed without the extra blanket and mothers made do with very little in the kitchen. Life was difficult. I remember Grandfather's stories about life growing up during this time.

In 1928, just before the Depression, William and his family of six lived in Missouri in a simple

This is the chicken farm that William called home. Above is a closer view of the two-story hay barn and the family chickens.

white house on a three-acre chicken farm. With five thousand chickens, they made a living selling eggs, shipping them by train to Barnes Hospital in St. Louis. They had a root cellar under the old white house where they kept the milk, cream, potatoes, and cheese. In the fields, they grew alfalfa. The family garden grew corn, tomatoes, carrots, turnips, and grapes. But it was the two-story hay barn which Grandpa thought was the most exciting place. It was filled with hay, pet snakes, and a cow.

Many of the surrounding farms were slowly abandoned during the Depression because farmers couldn't afford to stay. The income from their crops was just not enough to live on.

"Families all over just moved away." Grandfather said. "To California, mostly."

Though money was scarce and the economy was failing, Grandfather said that he never once felt poor. Even though his bathing suit had holes in it, he still had one, and even though his food didn't come in a big assortment, he still ate at every meal. William always had the support of a family who loved him, and most importantly, a relationship with the one true God who created him, saved him, and who took care of every detail of his life. This gave William wealth far greater than money could offer. He once told me years later, "I didn't let the problems of our nation discourage my expectations of life. But I also knew what was required of me... hard work, a good attitude, and a thankful heart."

William was about eleven years old when his father was offered a job in Texas as a minister of a small country church. So in 1933, the Brown family moved to Cleburne, Texas. Although it was a small town, to William and his siblings it seemed like a big city compared to the country farm they had known all their lives. From 1933 to 1938, they moved several times as their father ministered in different churches. Times were hard. Money was scarce. The Depression wasn't over. Many times, William's father was paid with baskets of vegetables from someone's garden or eggs from the chickens. But these hard times were part of God's plan for molding your great-great-grandfather and preparing him for the special mission that lay ahead. And he felt this, even as a boy:

A Depression breadline

-- 14 --

"My father would treat me to a scoop of Butter Pecan ice cream. We would go while I was on break from my job at the shoe shop in town, but it happened only every once in a while. As a sixteen-year-old boy, I realized how special those times were, just the two of us. Pop and I would talk about life, dreams, and goals. It was during talks like these that I realized there was more to life than just living for myself. God required a lot from me. Every day was to be lived for Him. God had given me my father as a role model. When I saw the kind of man he was, I wanted to be like that. My father taught me that selfishness doesn't get a person anywhere, and that because Christ had died for us, we had a mission. A mission to the Cross in humility. When a person is humble, there is no room for selfishness. Little did I know that there would soon be a time when I would have the opportunity to give of myself."

Across the Pacific Ocean, the Depression was affecting Germany. Most of their economy was built on foreign trade. They depended on other countries for many of the things they needed. America was one of the most dependable. When our economy fell, the Germans felt the effects. It happened like this: An American company would go bankrupt from the stock-market crash and have to let all its employees go. The men who lost their jobs now had no money to buy things such as shoes. This caused the shoe salesman to lose his job because

no one was buying! Now the shoe store isn't buying shoes from
the company in Germany that made the shoes and sold them to
America; so all of those workers in Germany lose their jobs
too. This happened in many industries.

The German people began to lose money, supplies, food,
jobs--it scared them. They needed a solution to these growing
problems. They were willing to trust anybody who could give
them hope, even if that hope was based on lies.

Now remember this, children: When men do not look to God
for answers, Satan is always there, ready to give lies. Many
of the German people did not look to God. Instead they looked
to an evil, hateful man named Adolph Hitler. Hitler wanted to
take over the world, and he would lie, cheat, steal, and kill
in order to do it.

Because Grandfather was a young boy, he didn't fully
understand all that was going on with Hitler in Germany, but
he knew it was serious. His father, who was a minister, took
him to meetings with other ministers to discuss the war that
had broken out in Europe and in Asia. At that point in time,

America was trying its hardest to stay out of the conflict. But we were beginning to wonder if Hitler's reign of terror would spread to our beloved country.

The Japanese were fighting on the side of the Germans, and on December 7, 1941, they bombed our naval base at Pearl Harbor in Hawaii. Once our homeland was attacked, we could avoid war no longer.

America had to defend herself. We had no choice, now, but to fight, and fight to win, to protect our freedom, to protect our future. Our boys were ready. They understood hard work and sacrifice. The boys who became soldiers had grown up learning that when hard times came, they had to work with a willing heart. Only God had known that they needed the Depression to prepare them. So when war hit and we were in trouble, they did what they had done before. They made sacrifices and worked hard. This time, their nation's freedom was at stake.

Your great-great-grandfather was one of the thousands of men who fought, who sacrificed, who experienced things we can't even imagine. Pay attention, children. Ponder these words, for most of these great men are dead, and their stories are being lost. The legacy they left can be yours, but you must know and appreciate what they did. You must understand how this war, their sacrifice, changed our country, our lives, your life, forever.

Jewish people were terribly persecuted by the Nazis

"So teach us to number our days,
That we may gain a heart of wisdom."

Psalm 90:12

Chapter 2

Children, picture in your mind a young man you know, about eighteen, nineteen, and twenty years old. Imagine him being far away from home, training all day long for weeks and months, marching for hours in the hot sun, learning how to sail ships and fly planes. He must learn how to obey without question, prepare to fight a powerful enemy, and maybe to die. That was what young William, your great-great-grandfather, and hundreds of other young men like him faced.

In December of 1942, when William was nineteen, he joined the Army Air Corps. He had finished one year of college when he decided that his education would have to wait, because there was something more important for him to do.

"My country was at war. There was no room for thinking of what I wanted for my life. The future of my children and their children, the morals of my country, and the way our lives would be lived was at stake. My country needed me. 'Self' was the price of freedom."

So, William and a few of his friends went to Fort Bliss in
El Paso, Texas to join the military. The first step was taking
an aptitude test. Can you picture the scene: A small, hot
room filled with wooden desks, boys crammed in, and probably
very quiet. Even with so many people, there wouldn't be a
lot of carefree conversation. More than anything, I imagine
stillness. Stillness and waiting....

Then a voice of authority said:

"Please men, take a seat. The tests are on the desks in
front of you. When you have finished, exit the door to the
left of the room. Your results will be posted within the day."

The test was not a problem for William, even with only one
year of college.

"My buddies and I had been pretty juiced up in academics.
We weren't brilliant, but we knew enough to do well on the
test. After we were accepted, they gave us the choice of going
to Europe or Japan. We could fly bombers or fighter planes.
They made my destination Japan... my occupation, a Fighter
Pilot."

With that, his training
began. Your great-great-
grandfather had to be two
things in order to survive
the difficult training
ahead. First, he had to
be teachable. Second, he
had to be obedient. If he
had decided at any time to
do things his own way, it
would have been over for

him. William learned to have respect for his leaders, even when the work was hard and the rules were strict.

Mornings came early for all the cadets. At 4:00 a.m., drill sergeants would come into their quarters for inspection, looking for anything out of place. The cadets were required to keep their sheets so tight that if they dropped a coin on the bed, the coin would bounce. If the coin didn't bounce, the bed was stripped. The cadets' shoes had to be polished so well that they could almost see their faces in them. Mistakes cost them greatly. One consequence was having to stand guard for several hours through the night with an empty gun. Can you imagine how tired they would be the next day through more training?

Cadet William E. Brown, 1943

I can remember Grandfather saying once that they were made to stand at attention for two hours. They stood still while a pilot lectured on flying techniques. The heat was unbearable; boys all over the yard were falling. It took everything in them to stand completely still, with their arms down, shoulders back, and knees locked.

"The key was to relax our shoulders and neck. Also, a consistent breathing pattern would help us to have control, and help us relax a little. Being a cadet was no joke. There was nothing fun about it. We weren't there for pleasure. The work was as much as a man could stand. Discipline became every man's middle name. Every day of basic training was the same. Drills, drills, drills.... Our cadet group moved about four different times in one year, using equipment and facilities all over Texas. Each town had a different name, but the routine was the same. The town of Ballinger, however, was a welcome and special treat. It was a small Texas town. The people in this town were wonderful. On one of the nights we were there, they fixed a meal for us, a real meal. They used real china, real silver forks and knives, glass cups, and made real home-cooked food. Just like mama cooks. There was fresh meat and vegetables and delicious desserts. They made us feel so loved and appreciated. It was a wonderful way to let us know they were thinking of us as we prepared for combat.... I will always remember their kindness.

"From Ballinger, Texas, we took short 'cross-countries'-- short trips from one airport to another. The first time I ever landed on a cement strip was in Coleman, another small town. That was a different feeling after just landing on dirt for so long. From there we went to San Angelo to do night flying. We would take our planes out at dusk and fly through the night. We did our night training in a big plane called a BT-13. If I had had the choice, I would have chosen to go out on my missions in the BT-13 because it was stronger than the P-51. It could take a lot of damage before going down. The P-51 wasn't as tough. The most fascinating thing about flying in the dark to me was that I could see the fire coming out of my engine ports like big blowtorches in the air."

Finally, the Army Air Corps sent William by boat to Oahu, Hawaii, where he joined the 45th fighter squadron. This, children, is where your great-great-grandfather really learned how to fly. The 45th fighter squadron had just returned from combat. They had been sent to train new pilots. William was one of those pilots. He said he had never seen anyone fly like those guys did.

"They trained us well," William said. "The day they took us up to learn to fly in formation in P-47s was the day we became real flyers. We had a great captain whose name was Art Bridge. He taught us a lot about discipline, and about doing our jobs. I came to realize my importance because if I didn't do well it would mess up the other formation flyers in the air with me. My actions affected the pilots around me."

Never once did the trainees stop learning. Every day they practiced something new: from learning to land at high speeds to studying how to hit a target from the air while flying sideways. It took days and weeks of training. William and his group were in Oahu, Hawaii for about six months, training in P-51 Mustangs, the planes they would fly into combat.

In 1944, Grandfather was commissioned Second Lieutenant.
Being commissioned is similar to graduating from college.
There is a ceremony and all the lieutenants are lined up.
Each man is pinned with a badge that will signify his rank and he is given a certificate proving that he has completed his training. William's parents came to see him graduate. It was hard for them to watch him that day. I'm sure they had mixed feelings, being proud of his accomplishments and his willingness to fight for his country, but at the same time feeling anxious about the thought of losing him. They knew that his life was at great risk and that they might never see him again.

"My parents were afraid, yes. But they both believed in a God who was not afraid. My father was always reminding me to say to myself over and over before

My grandfather upon being
commissioned 2nd. Lt.

heading into danger, 'The Lord has gone before me.' My father believed that if you told yourself this often, it would make a lot of life's troubles easier to handle. He was right! If I kept my mind full of the idea that God knows what I'm about to face and will go through it with me, there's not much room for being scared. How can you be scared when you know that the God of the entire universe is right there with you!"

William's training was complete. He had worked hard for two years. He was ready to fight the enemy. Physically he was strong enough; mentally, he knew how to respond to different situations; and spiritually, his heart was right before God. There was no doubt in his mind where he would go if anything were to happen to his physical body. He was ready for whatever lay ahead. There was no fear. God had gone before him, remember?

"In the day when I cried out,
You answered me,

And made me bold with
strength in my soul."

Psalm 138:3

Chapter 3

Although William and the other soldiers were well trained,
nothing could prepare them for the horror they would face.
Although my grandfather knew that God was with him, the pain
of having to experience such trauma was very real. In the
winter of 1945, my grandfather's unit was sent to the island
of Iwo Jima. Dear children, it was on this island that one of
the bloodiest battles of the Second World War was fought.

"I will never forget the first time I stepped onto the
island of Iwo Jima," Grandfather told me. "We all unloaded
and paused for a minute. Everyone stopped to look around at
the scene. From where we were, we could see hospital tents on
the west beach and soldiers everywhere; some were lying down,
others standing. About one hundred yards away, over near the
edge of the airport, I saw about two dozen marines. They were
completely exhausted; they had been on the front lines, and
they had come back to get some sleep, I guess. Their clothing
was dirty and tattered. Their faces were dejected. Some

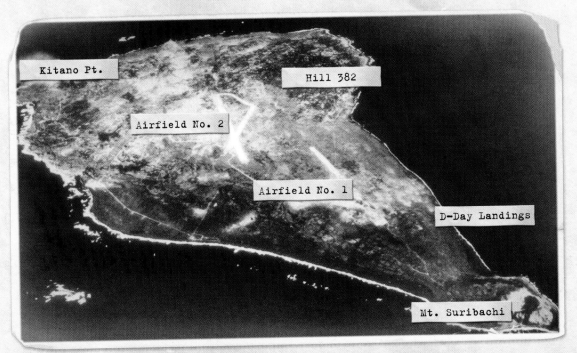

A map of Iwo Jima and the two airfields where William landed

were just sitting, some lying on the ground. It was a moving picture that reminded me of the sacrifice--of the horror--of war. I knew the minute I stepped foot on Iwo Jima that what we were about to face was serious, and it was not going to be without pain."

Let me give you a little history of this island. Iwo Jima is one of a string of islands off the coast of Japan, an island owned by the Japanese. During the war, it became very important because of its location. At 660 miles south of Tokyo, it was midway between the mainland of Japan and the American B-29 bases on Saipan. There were two landing strips on the wider part of the island and America needed these airstrips for P-51 mustang fighters like your great-great-grandfather's. If our pilots could land on the island, they could escort our big bombers, protecting them on their raids against Japan. The island could also be used for emergency

landings by damaged planes flying back from Japan. America
needed to capture this island. We needed Iwo Jima, and the
Japanese knew it. So, for two and a half months, Army, Navy,
and Marine Corps planes dropped five hundred-pound bombs
on the island. Before long, Iwo Jima began looking like the
surface of the moon.

Finally, D-Day arrived. At two minutes after nine o'clock
on the morning of February 19, 1945, our Marines landed on Iwo's
beaches. Thirty thousand Marines struggled ashore that day.
Long, horrible battles were fought, killing thousands of men.

On D-plus-four, a group of Marines climbed the northern
part of Mount Suribachi, the highest point on the
island. At the top, they raised a small flag, hoping to
encourage fellow soldiers with America's inspiring
symbol, but found the flag was too small. A few
Marines struggled down and back again to find a
bigger flag. A young man named Joe Rosenthal took
a photograph of this second flag raising. His
photograph became the most famous image of
the Second World War.

The flag raising was a great
encouragement to the Americans on Iwo
Jima, but it did not mark the end of
the battle. There were thirty-three
more days of intense fighting
before Suribachi was secure.

Many of the Japanese
wore explosive charges
strapped to their bodies
and blew themselves
up in order to kill

more American
soldiers. Understand
this children, that
the enemy is willing
to do anything it
takes to win.

Hand-to-hand
combat was
common. The
living conditions
were seemingly
unbearable. Most
of the men lived
in foxholes or
tunnels dug into the
ground. Whole hills
were hollowed out and
reconstructed from the
inside. Some of them were
big enough to hold four
hundred soldiers.

"The first night in our
foxholes," William remembered,
"was one of constant explosions.
The island was lit up like a thousand
fireflies swirling in a jar. The skies
for at least a thousand feet up were
filled with smoke and dust. I believe
there was a battle going on, on the
northern part of the island, but in a
short while we grew used to the sounds of
war. By the next night, we had no problem
falling asleep amidst the noise."

The temperature at night was a cold forty to forty-five degrees. During the day it was hot and muggy. Many of the men struggled with sicknesses from lack of nourishment. Portions were small and sometimes hardly edible. Some of the flight surgeons wouldn't allow their pilots to fly until they had been given tents to live in and cafeteria food to eat. The men needed basic care in order to fly their planes skillfully and safely.

The island was full of spiders. Soldiers sleeping on the ground made easy targets for bites which spread disease and infection. To kill off the bugs and vermin, C-47s would fly over the island dumping clouds of insecticide. But Grandfather said that it was hard to breathe sometimes with all of the insecticide and bomb smoke blowing around all of the time.

"At times, we would just sit in our holes, waiting for the air to clear. My squadron was given tents to sleep in after about ten days of being on the island. I felt safer being in my hole in the ground though. It was harder to breathe down there, and one could easily become claustrophobic, but with all the surprise night attacks by the enemy, I felt insecure sleeping above ground.

A B-29 crashed into the airfield, destroying several planes in William's squadron

"Every day I lost a friend, sometimes more than one a day. I remember telling myself not to allow this to affect me. There was no time for me to think about the loss of a comrade. There was no time for me to feel sorry. I couldn't look back. I had to look forward. I couldn't carry all of the deaths of Iwo Jima with me. Many days there was no feeling in my heart at all. Any ounce of emotion that had been left in my head by the horrors of the war didn't make its way to my heart. I had to come to a point where I didn't feel anything. I couldn't. It's almost like my mind was in shock. The reality of it came to me later. Death became just like the fighting. It became routine. I didn't consider death. I only wondered why I had been spared.

"I had been assigned to fly on my birthday, January 8, 1945, but I asked to take a holiday. My captain gave me the day off. The mission I missed encountered some clouds that day, and the planes ran together and crashed in the ocean. All of the pilots were killed. When I returned to base I was informed of the deaths. I would have gone down with the rest that day had God permitted it."

As my grandfather said, he only wondered why his life had been spared.

Children, we always think of men as being strong and brave, and this is true; but there are still times when it is right and proper for them to pause and feel pain. One day while your great-great-grandfather was on the island, he visited Iwo Jima's cemetery. I can only imagine the pain and sorrow that must have flooded his heart and his eyes as he gazed upon the thousands of crosses that blanketed the dusty grounds. As my grandfather stood there, alone with God and with the memories of the men who had given their all, he couldn't help but be filled with thankfulness; thankfulness that God had saved him

from an eternal death. He knew that any day his life could
be taken away from him. But he also realized that his life
was not his own. It had been given to him by God as a gift.
Furthermore, he knew that if he were to die, it wouldn't be
a real death. Sure, his physical body would stop working,
but his spirit would only move on. Everlasting life had been
promised him after death because he had put his faith in the
sacrifice made by Jesus Christ for his sins.

The last day of the battle for Iwo Jima was March 26, 1945.
We were victorious. Because of the ultimate sacrifice by
almost seven thousand American Marines, more than 25,000 lives
were saved during the next five months. American control of
the island allowed 2,251 emergency landings of aircraft which
would have otherwise crashed in the Pacific Ocean.

"Whenever I am afraid,
I will trust in You.

In God (I will praise His word),

In God I have put my trust;
I will not fear.

What can flesh do to me?"

Psalm 56:3-4

Chapter 4

I would like to describe to you exactly what your great-great-grandfather did while serving in World War II. I've told you that he was in the Army Air Corps, but let me explain what he did as a fighter pilot. His primary duty was to escort missions to Honshu and Kyushu in Japan. When our men went out to drop a bomb or to attack a specific place, they would fly together in groups. They were sometimes called "missions" and sometimes called "raids." The bomber would be escorted by other planes flying beside, above, and below it to protect the bomber from enemy fire. Grandfather flew a P-51 Mustang on his missions. Mustangs have six fifty-caliber machine guns in their wings and carry a five hundred-pound bomb full of an explosive called napalm. My grandfather's job was to escort those bombers and shoot the enemy if they attacked. Most of his missions lasted six to eight hours. Afterwards, he would follow the bomber back to Iwo Jima.

"Every once in a while," Grandfather said, "my squadron would get night patrol. Some of us guys would go up about

thirty minutes early and we would practice by having
individual combat. We would try and get on each other's
tails. It was important to be able to quickly get right up
behind somebody. It was one of the harder things to do, so we
would practice with each other. Some were really good at it,
and others weren't so good."

Look at the pictures I've included in my letter to you
children. Do you see the planes? It surely would take a great
deal of faith on the pilot's part to trust that the plane
would do what it was supposed to do while in the air. Many
times, smoke or clouds would obscure the pilot's vision. A
pilot must trust his instruments. In certain circumstances,
his senses can become confused. He feels that he is flying
right side up when really he is flying upside down. His senses
may confuse him, but his flying instruments won't lie.

A person's relationship with God is like the pilot and
his instruments. In the same way that a pilot must trust his

plane's instruments when everything in his body tells him the opposite, so a Christian must trust what God says no matter what he feels. Even when it doesn't make sense, or when he is confused, or when he thinks he knows what's best, he must trust his instruments. How many pilots, I wonder, have lost their lives from lack of trust in their instruments? And how many followers of Christ have lost their way from lack of obedience to the written Word of God? Do you see how they relate? Sometimes we are unwilling to submit ourselves to what God wants to do with our lives because we think we know what is best. Yet we are called to obey, even when we don't understand what God is doing. Even when our future is unclear to us, we must trust that God knows what He is doing... because He does.

The next time you see a plane and its pilot, and as you look upon the greatness and power of the machine, I hope you will be reminded of the greatness and power of God. When you look at the pilot and see how small he is compared to his plane, think about how that man is putting his faith in the accuracy of the instruments as the plane takes him into the sky. Then think about how much you and I are like that pilot, putting our faith in God, as He takes us on our journey.

I want to tell you another story to give you an even better idea of what these pilots faced. When I asked my grandfather to describe the first time he saw a Japanese plane in the air with him, this is what he said:

"The first time I encountered an enemy plane, I was covering a submarine over Kyushu. Every once in a while, they would send me out to 'cover.' Say one of our submarines is in enemy territory, depending on the situation, and what our guys were doing, they would need someone to look out for them, above water. In this case, our submarine was heading towards

a kamikaze base in Japan. I remember looking down and seeing
an enemy plane flying right under me. Of course, I wanted to
follow him and shoot him, but couldn't. I was protecting a
submarine. I saw another one, and then another! Thankfully
I was not by myself. There were a few other planes covering
with me. I realized as they danced around under us that they
were trying to distract us from our job. They slowly started
flying away, hoping that we would follow them. Their goal
was to lure us away from the submarine. It didn't work. We
stayed."

   Always remember, children, that the enemy will try its
hardest to distract us from our mission.

"Save me, O God!
For the waters have come up to my neck.

I sink in deep mire,
Where there is no standing;

I have come into deep waters,
Where the floods overflow me.

I am weary with my crying;
My throat is dry;

My eyes fail while I wait for my God."

Psalm 69:1-3

Chapter 5

Can you remember an absolutely gorgeous day? The sky is the bluest you've ever seen. It's as clear as glass. The temperature is perfect, and everything about it makes you glad you are alive. This is the kind of day it was off the shores of Iwo Jima, and throughout Tokyo Bay, on May 29, 1945. Imagine just a slight breeze and a big, beautiful, bright sun. What a perfect day for flying. What a day to remember. Although this day will never be forgotten in the mind of my grandfather, it is not because of the beauty of the sky. Let me explain:

William woke up early that morning to prepare for an important mission. There were 450 B-29s and one hundred Mustangs that were to fly to Yokahama. Can you picture those hundreds of airplanes taking off, one after the other, as the sun rose in the sky? What an amazing sight that must have been!

Our men had a successful fight against the enemy. The day was going well, the mission was accomplished, and our men

were heading back to Iwo Jima. The 550 planes planned
to split into groups to make it easier and safer to travel.
So, everyone divided up to return to the island--everyone,
that is, except William, who encountered one last Japanese
Zero. He and his flight leader engaged this enemy plane,
shooting at him, when all of a sudden there was no sound--my
grandfather's engine had stopped!

   "My flight leader just disappeared in the sky somewhere.
I looked around and I couldn't find the Zero we had been
shooting at," Grandfather explained to me. "I pushed the
plane over as much as I could, mustering as much speed as
possible. I got my engine started. I began gliding south,
from Tokyo Bay. Within a few minutes I saw some B-29s
returning from my same mission. I tried to get as far away
from them as I could. They were on my side but from where
I was, I figured I might be mistaken for an enemy plane.
Obviously I didn't get far enough away because, before I knew
it, I felt a jolt like you wouldn't believe and my engine
started to smoke. My instrument panel started flying apart,

and the gas caps popped up. I had been hit. The plane caught
on fire. I knew it was time to get out. We had been trained
on how to get out of an aircraft in an emergency, but when I
tried turning the plane upside down so that I could drop out
with my parachute, I couldn't drop! I decided to roll it back
up, put it in a slight climb, and crawl out the right side.
I had heard stories of guys crawling out and getting blown
into the tail. Many pilots had died tragically that way.
Thankfully, when I did manage to crawl out, I slid right by
the tail without getting bumped.

"I'll never forget being told about one month before my
accident that they had tested a dozen chutes from our squadron
by putting sandbags on them and then dumping them out of a
plane over a field and that half of those parachutes didn't
open! The chutes that some of our guys had jumped with on
previous missions didn't billow. It worried our superiors that
chutes weren't opening, but there was nothing they could do!

"Well, my parachute did open, and I floated right down into
the ocean. I guess I was at about eight thousand feet. On my
way down, I passed through some clouds, an experience I can't
even begin to describe. I could see everything from up there.
I was able to spot a little Japanese island a few miles to
the side, and I saw the little circle that my plane made when
it hit the water. Seeing your plane hit the water like that
really does something to you. It leaves this lump in your
stomach as you realize that the airplane you had been in only
seconds ago is now sinking to the bottom of the ocean.

"During training in Richmond, Virginia, we had been taught
how to inflate our life rafts in swimming pools. I had
practiced and practiced, so doing it again in the ocean was a
piece of cake. After the boat had been inflated, I crawled in
and took off my shoes. The big question at the moment was: am

I too close to that Japanese island to set off my smoke bombs? Did I want to take the chance of being seen by the Japanese? I decided to chance it. I set off two. After waiting for nearly fifteen minutes, I set off the rest of them. I must have sat in my boat, waiting, for close to two hours. Sitting there, I realized I had been cut on the left side of my neck. Shrapnel or a piece of my plane must have hit me. The salt water was good for it though. It eased the pain and slowed down the bleeding."

When I asked my grandfather if he was afraid, if he was in shock, or if he was exhausted, he said, "No, it's not easy to describe though. I think the best way to say it is that you just take it one step at a time."

He was right! It wouldn't have helped him any to worry about what could happen to him if he were captured. He needed, more than anything, to stay calm. Having his thoughts in a hundred different places at once wasn't going to help him focus on what was going on right then, at that moment. He had been trained how to respond. All he needed to do was follow through with what he knew to be right. The last thing he wanted to do was to panic. I'm sure there was a moment of shock as he realized that his plane had just been blown up, but at the same time, part of him was ready for it. In the Army Air Corps, men were trained to expect these things. This was war. They couldn't afford to forget that... and my grandfather didn't.

No one is sure whether the flares that were set off were seen by our men or if someone saw his plane being hit and radioed him in. However it happened... it did happen. Praise the Lord. I cannot even begin to imagine the feelings of relief and utter thankfulness that my grandfather must have felt in his heart when his fellow Americans rescued him.

"I guess I could've been in a sort of daze," He told me. "I was just sitting there looking off into the sky when I turned around and all of a sudden, there, right beside me was the most wonderful sight I had ever seen. A submarine! I hadn't even noticed it coming up!"

William was rescued by the U.S.S. Pipefish

"Tell me, Grandfather!" I had asked him. "Did you know right away that it was an American sub? What kind of thoughts were running through your mind as they pulled up to you?"

My grandfather went on to tell me that he did not recognize the submarine at first, but very quickly came to realize that it was American. It all happened so fast. When a submarine comes up out of the water, it must complete its task as quickly as possible. Submarines are too easily seen by planes.

"I was so excited by the time I realized these were our men coming to rescue me that I left my shoes in the raft when I climbed into the sub. They were my good shoes, too! As I reached up to take the hand of the Navy officer helping me in, it was all I could do to keep myself under control, I was so relieved. The feeling of being rescued, saved, protected... it's not something you can describe, really, but it's one of the greatest feelings that one can have. As long as I live, I will never forget that moment, when I took the hand of one of my rescuers, and was lifted up... into safety."

My dear, dear grandchildren, as I ponder the rescue story of William, my grandfather, your great-great-grandfather, I cannot help but be reminded of how much my rescue story is so like his. I was stranded in an ocean all alone, just like Grandfather, except the ocean I was in was an ocean of sin,

not water. I was surrounded by an enemy whose goal was the corruption of my soul.

There was only one way that my grandfather could be saved. It was not by trying to swim to shore. He would have drowned from exhaustion. It was not by living the rest of his life out on the water in that small life raft. He would have starved to death or been killed in a storm. There was absolutely nothing he could do to save himself from certain death. His only hope was that someone who cared enough would come to save him.

This applies to my rescue story as well. There was only one way that I could be sure of safety--only one way I could be taken out of the horrible sea of sin. That was through Jesus Christ, who was holy and without sin, and who cared enough to come and save my life. When the submarine rose out of the water, opened its door, and offered a hand to my grandfather, he didn't have to think for a second if he really wanted to be rescued. At that moment there was nothing more important to him than being saved. It was the same for me. Christ came to me in my ocean of sin, reached out His hand to save me, and all I could do was receive His offer.

I feel the same way my grandfather did when he said that there are no words to express the feeling he had once he was saved. It is indescribable, and I believe it's the greatest feeling that a human being can have. I will never forget being rescued by Christ, and I will never be able to repay Him for what He did.

Children, more than anything, I want you to have a rescue story like mine. I want you to realize that, without Jesus Christ, you are lost in an ocean of sin. There is no hope for you, unless He saves you.

"Forever, O Lord, Your word is settled in heaven.

Your faithfulness endures to all generations;
You established the earth, and it abides.

They continue this day according to Your ordinances,
For all are Your servants.

Unless Your law had been my delight,
I would then have perished in my affliction.

I will never forget Your precepts,
For by them You have given me life."

Psalm 119:89-93

Chapter 6

Throughout this letter, I have tried to show you that what my grandfather did--what all of the men of this war did-- was for you and for me. It is very important that we not take their sacrifice for granted. They fought for something that is worth fighting for, something that has been given to us as a gift from God; a gift that needs to be protected because so often man tries to take it away. It is a gift that needs to be taken seriously because too often we fail to understand its importance and the cost it exacted. That gift is freedom.

You see, your great-great-grandfather wanted you to be able to have the freedom to speak what you think. He wanted you to be able to publicly declare your views about life and God. He wanted you boys to have the freedom to choose for yourselves the kinds of jobs you will have someday, in order to support your families. He wanted you to live in a country without the fear of persecution regarding what you believe, to be free to worship the way you desire to worship. He wanted you and me to live in a land without want.

My grandfather believed that this is what God intended. He believed that these were gifts given to man by God. The only problem is that, because of sin, these gifts will always be under attack. All over the world people are suffering under the authority of a man or a government that will not allow them to choose what they would do with their lives. This causes the people to struggle. The things they work hard for are taken away from them. Because of sin, man's desire is to take control of freedom, so that he can then control people's lives. This is what the men of World War II saw as a possibility. This is what they fought to prevent. Hundreds of thousands of young men, most of them just boys, gave their lives for this cause. They decided that even the breath that was in them was worth giving, if it meant they could preserve the freedom of their children and their children's children.

I want you to understand how important it was to them, and how important it should be to you. When I think about all the different stories I have heard of the men who fought, I am overwhelmed at what they were willing to do... for us. I think the question now becomes: how willing would we be to do what they did? Only God knows, but there may come a time when our freedom must be fought for once again. It is extremely important that we pass on to our children the legacy that has been left by the thousands of men who died. My desire is that you would someday pass down this story to your children.

Ponder the faithfulness of God to your great-great-grandfather. God chose to bless him by giving him a son who walked faithfully with God, just like he did. His son then had a daughter, whose desire is to seek the face of the Lord also. I am that daughter. This generational faithfulness to God was lived out in your great grandfather's family because he passed on what God was doing in his life. He taught his son the ways of the Lord. My grandfather made clear to my father that the only reason he survived World War II was because God wanted it that way. It wasn't good works or the fact that he was a good man that saved him. Truthfully, he was a sinner, a sinner who didn't deserve to be saved either out of that big blue ocean off of Tokyo Bay or out of his ocean of sin. Openly, he gave all of the credit to the Lord. I pray that your hearts will be open to receiving the offer of rescue, of salvation, that Christ extends to you. Then, I want you to be willing to share your rescue story with your children, so that they might not forget that God is faithful to those who love Him.

Dear ones, my fire is burning low now and the light from the flames is growing dim. I will bring my letter to a close, but I will leave you with this: Never ever forget that freedom is not free. It will always come at a great price. Never ever forget the men who gave their lives because they understood that so well. And never ever forget that God is faithful to those who pass down the stories of God's work in their lives. You have been called... I have been called. With the help of the Almighty, Sovereign God, I believe we will have a witness that is powerful.

With all of my love to you,

Grandmother

Bill and Mary Brown

People talk about what big sacrifices we made as soldiers. What looked like sacrifice was really our opportunity to live out those principles that Jesus clearly demonstrated. Don't always take the easy way. Be discerning. Be wise.

Out of God's grace, He kept me alive. He is to be praised. He brought me a wife and a family. God sought me and gave me an opportunity to serve Him.

Praise be the Lord!

Bill Brown

Epilogue

William Brown flew eighteen missions to Japan and was shot down over Tokyo Bay on May 29, 1945. The war did not end until August of that same year. After being picked up by the submarine "Pipefish," he was taken to Guam. William was there for about four days before he was taken back to Iwo Jima in a C-47.

After arriving at Iwo Jima, William was sent out to Hickam Field, Honolulu. It was a rest camp where he stayed for some time. By the time he was released, the war had come to an end, and he was sent home on a cargo ship that traveled to San Francisco. As they pulled in and went under the bridge, he heard a military band playing songs on the dock, songs like "Sentimental Journey." William never forgot that moment when he arrived home. He was proud to be an American.

As soon as William had been shot down, the military reported that he had been killed in action. His few belongings back on Iwo Jima were divided among his fellow soldiers and a telegram was brought by a soldier to his parents informing them that he had been killed. Three weeks passed before they were informed that he was alive and on his way home.

William returned to Texas and finished college. There he met his beautiful wife, Mary. They were married December 23,1947.

Comin' In on a Wing and a Prayer

The song, "Comin' In on a Wing and a Prayer"—with lyrics by Harold Adamson and music by Jimmy McHugh—came out at the end of 1942. One of William Brown's personal favorites during the War, the song quickly became a sensational hit on both sides of the Atlantic.

One of our planes was missing
Two hours overdue
One of our planes was missing
With all its gallant crew
The radio sets were humming
We waited for a word
Then a noise broke
Through the humming
    and this is what we heard

Comin' in on a wing and a prayer
Comin' in on a wing and a prayer
Though there's one motor gone
We can still carry on
Comin' in on a wing and a prayer

What a show, what a fight, boys
We really hit our target for tonight
How we sing as we limp through the air
Look below, there's our field over there
With just one motor gone
We can still carry on
Comin' in on a wing and a prayer

Comin' in on a wing and a prayer
Comin' in on a wing and a prayer
With our full crew on board
And our trust in the Lord
We're comin' in on a wing and a prayer

A World of Thanks

Thanks to all of my dear family at Trinity Baptist Church, for the support and amazing encouragement you gave to me as I penned this letter.

To my wonderful Grandparents—thank you both for the legacy that you have given me. God's richest blessings on you for your faithfulness to Him.

To my parents—Scott and Deborah Brown, you have inspired me with your lives to live for God's glory. I love you both with all my heart.

To Mr. Doug Phillips—who inspired me with the idea of writing this story down. Thank you for the effort you put into making this happen. I am forever indebted to you and I am so thankful for your friendship.